IMAGES
of London

WEMBLEY

History in the making: looking for Tudor and Medieval remains during the archaeological excavation at the Unigate Depot, Hundred Elms Farm, Sudbury in 1991.

IMAGES
of London

WEMBLEY

Geoffrey Hewlett

TEMPUS

To many the stadium, with its twin towers, *is* Wembley. Its construction eighty years ago heralded major changes for this suburb of north west London, just as the proposals for a new national stadium do today.

First published 2002

Tempus Publishing Limited
The Mill, Brimscombe Port,
Stroud, Gloucestershire, GL5 2QG

© Geoffrey Hewlett, 2002

British Library Cataloguing in Publication Data.
A catalogue record for this book is available from the British Library.

ISBN 0 7524 2633 8

Typesetting and origination by Tempus Publishing Limited
Printed in Great Britain by Midway Colour Print, Wiltshire

Contents

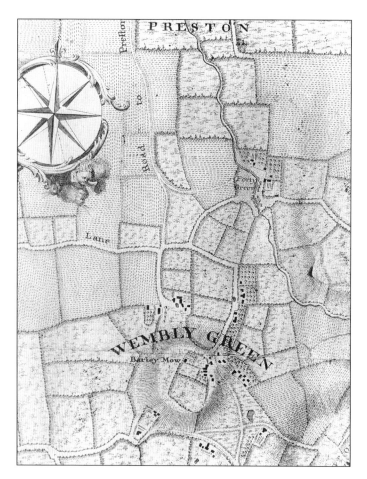

Map dated 1744 showing Wembley Park before it was a park. From John Rocque's *Map of London & Environs.*

Acknowledgements

I would like to extend my thanks firstly to those largely unknown individuals who over the years have recorded people and places, and those who have collected the results of such labours for posterity. Without that commitment, collections would not exist. In that role, the Wembley History Society and its members and supporters have performed an invaluable service over the past fifty years. This is the Society's Golden Anniversary year and a large number of photographs have been selected from its collection to add to the author's own archives. The Society's collection results from the accumulation of items donated by others and my thanks go to the many who have contributed to it, including in this case the *Wembley Observer* – its editor and readers, Brent Council's Environmental Services, the former Greater London Council, the Sir John Soane Museum, the Science Museum and Messrs. Ted Akester, Richard Brock, H.C. Casserley, J. Cumming, A. Dunn, Geoff Hoggett, Kenneth Jones, P. Madden, and Kuno Reitz.

Secondly, my thanks go to the London Borough of Brent, and in particular to Ian Johnston and colleagues in the Borough's Archives for their assistance and permission to publish photographs in their collection. Next, I record the help and guidance received from Simmons Aerofilms and from London's Transport Museum. Their copyright is acknowledged beside the photographs. Lastly, but by no means least, I thank my wife and sons for their encouragement while I've sat and pondered, or travelled in search of material.

Introduction

Wembley forms part of the administrative Borough of Brent in north west London. It is part of the inter-war suburban metropolis, yet its component parts – Alperton (from Ealhbeorht's farm); Preston (from the Priest's farm); and Tokyngton (from the farm of Toca's sons) recall villages of Saxon origin which were absorbed into London's expansion in the twentieth century. Thus, even as late as 1914, this was still an attractive country area, with leafy lanes, fields and farmhouses.

Wembley (from Wemba lea – Wemba's clearing in the forest- recalled in AD 825) had its origins on Wembley Hill, where the High Street still survives; yet until the early twentieth century it was of secondary importance to Sudbury – the south burgh (south that is of Harrow, the manor to which Wembley belonged). When the London to Birmingham railway passed through what is now Wembley Central in 1837, the station which was subsequently opened in 1844 was called 'Sudbury', as that was the nearest hamlet of consequence. The quadrupling of rail tracks in 1870 and the provision of local rail services gave rise in 1877 to a hotel, and by 1882 to a parade of shops in what is now the west end of the High Road. The roads which crossed the railway at Wembley and North Wembley had been replaced by bridges by about 1839. The church of St John at Wembley was erected in 1845, close to Barham Park where Wembley's benefactors, the Copland family, lived. Real development did not commence until the 1890s. The death of the local land owner released building land for sale whilst the Great Central Railway, built across Wembley Hill, opened a station there in 1906 and encouraged further building along the High Road. Wembley's population of 203 in 1851 had reached 48,500 in 1931, by which time the adjoining local centres were also undergoing rapid change. Preston's earlier history was subordinate to the fortunes of Uxendon Manor house whose occupants, the Bellamy family, were arrested for treason in the Babington plot of 1586. Perhaps the most famous resident of Preston was John Lyon, who lived on what is now Preston Hill, and who not only founded Harrow School in 1572 but also gave money for its upkeep and, by bequest, provided for the repair of the Edgware and Harrow Roads. The Metropolitan Railway passed through Preston in 1880 but a station proposed there in 1896 was rejected because there were not enough residents. However, the rifle shooting competition of the 1908 Olympic Games was held at Uxendon Farm, Preston, and a halt appeared on Preston Road in 1908. A station did not materialise until 1933.

And so it was that much of the area's development was facilitated by improvements to and the growth of London's transport. Sudbury's expansion was sparked off by the coming of the Metropolitan District Railway (1903), the Great Central Railway (1905/06) and the trams (1910), for which the Sudbury 'Swan' was the terminus. The tram took about forty minutes to reach Sudbury from Paddington and between a six and ten minute service was provided. Giving the working classes access to the countryside by a cheap and rapid means of transport was greeted by some of the locals with mixed feelings!

Alperton's early development stemmed from the industrial revolution. The Paddington branch of the Grand Junction Canal, opened in 1801, particularly affected Alperton where brick and tile making flourished in the middle of the nineteenth century. Apart from handling the shipment of sand, gravel and coal (and later refuse), the canal transported hay to London and carried passenger traffic on pleasure trips from the City to the Pleasure Boat pub at Alperton and back. A local entrepreneur, Henry Haynes (1831-1910), at one time owned seventy of the 100 buildings in the village and employed nearly the entire labour force of 150 people. In 1888 he issued his own coinage for spending in his own shops.

In medieval times, the nearest place of worship for the inhabitants of Wembley was Tokyngton chapel, which stood on the east side of Wembley Green, from possibly as early as the twelfth century until the Dissolution in May 1545. The chapel grounds formed part of the Tokyngton estate which, by 1835, had passed to Joseph Neeld, the MP for Chippenham from 1830 to 1856. In 1913 his nephew, Sir Audley Dallas Neeld (1848–1941), proposed to develop the estate on garden city lines. The main farmhouse, Oakington Manor Farm, was occupied between 1862 and 1883 by Sir Patrick Talbot, son-in-law to the Victorian Prime Minister, the Earl of Derby, and who played an active part in the life of Wembley.

Much of the ownership of Wembley though had been in the hands of the Page family, whose principal seat was Wembley House. A later Victorian house of that name lay on the south side of Wembley Green (now the site of Copland School). In the eighteenth century, this was superseded in preference to a large house called 'Wellers' which stood on the slopes of Wembley Hill. In 1792, Richard Page engaged the landscape architect Humphry Repton, who had recently laid out Brondesbury Park, to re-style his property as a country mansion and landscape its grounds. This was the origin of 'Wembly Park'. After 1887, the park was acquired by the Metropolitan Railway (who had opened their railway across it to Harrow in 1880) and who proposed to develop it as a recreation centre for London. Dominating the cricket pitches, running track and boating lake was the principal feature – a virtual replica of the Eiffel Tower. The tower was commenced but never completed and survived as 'Watkin's Folly' until its demolition in 1907. This beauty spot was selected by the Government for the site of the British Empire Exhibition of 1924-1925 which, apart from the destruction of Wembley Park's countryside, was primarily responsible for the rapid development of the district. Approximately twenty-seven million people visited the Exhibition and local roads were widened and straightened for improved access by bus and car. Whilst many sought to settle in the charming countryside around and local builders busied themselves in transforming fields into suburban estates, the Exhibition also brought with it the National Stadium. This was finished ahead of time so that it could be opened for the Cup Final of 1923 and in the process assured for Wembley international recognition. Now the name of 'Wembley' is known world wide and its growth from village to suburb at the beginning of this process is recorded in the photographs which follow.

Geoffrey Hewlett
May 2002

One
Alperton

The early development of Alperton affected what was an isolated and scattered number of farms, houses, lodges and cottages. The coming of the canal in 1801 introduced industry, and changed the nature and frequency of visiting traffic but it wasn't until the coming of the railway in 1903 that a centre for Alperton was clearly established. This nineteenth century photograph of what could have been one of Alperton's by-ways is presumably that of Ealing Road, near the 'Chequers', called Brent Lane as it led down to the River Brent.

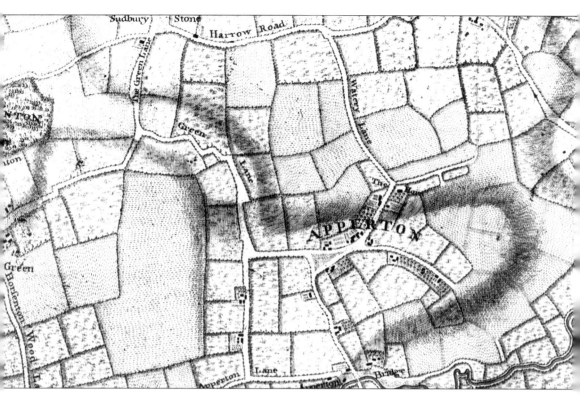

The map by John Rocque dated 1744, later embodied in his *Map of London & Environs* of 1746, shows the scattered form of Alperton (or 'Apperton' here). Green Lane became the basis of Bridgewater Road and Watery Lane became Ealing Road. Rocque was one of a family of immigrants from France. He practised land surveying and in 1737 began a survey of the whole of the built-up area of London to a scale of twenty-six inches to one mile. This was completed and published in 1746.

Opposite: The canal wharf in 1923. The Pelican barge, registered at Paddington, appears to be loading with gravel or clinker.

Alperton's expansion in the nineteenth century was the result of the growth of local industry. This was largely due to the opening of the Grand Junction Canal in 1801 and shipments of sand, gravel, coal, chalk rubbish and gas lime were soon commonplace activities.

Ealing Road canal bridge, c. 1900, seen from the Pleasure Boat. The Pleasure Boat public house in Ealing Road recalls the tourist trade. Whilst the canal transported hay to London, it brought to Alperton passenger traffic on pleasure trips from the City to the Pleasure Boat and back, boat going and returning 2s 6d (12.5p) each person. For the same price an 'unrivalled voyage' could be had from Alperton to Uxbridge and back.

Henry Haynes (1831–1910) shown here with his wife, Harriet, was principally a builder and brick-maker. At one time he owned about seventy of Alperton's 100 buildings and employed nearly the entire labour force, amounting to 150 people. In 1888 he issued his own private coinage for use in his shops. In 1866 his family moved from the Pleasure Boat to the new Alperton Park Hotel (now club premises) which then became his main residence.

Mount Pleasant, Alperton (formerly Honeypot Lane), *c.* 1900.

Wyatt's butchers shop on the east side of Ealing Road, near the Alperton Park Hotel. The smallest of the three men was Stanley Walden, the grandson of Henry Haynes.

This pre-1910 view of Gueran's, stationers, confectioners and tobacconists, records the shop which was at the corner of Ealing Road and Burns Road.

The Chequers public house on Ealing Road was called The Horn on Rocque's map of 1744. The present building was built in 1903 to designs by Stanley Hinge Hamp (1877–1968), the son of Thomas Hamp who moved to Alperton in 1886 and a partner in the architectural firm of Collcutt & Hamp. Stanley Hamp was later the architectural assessor of the competition for the design of Brent Town Hall and gave his name to Stanley Avenue.

Ealing Road, looking north-east from Alperton station in 1923. In the distance is the Alperton Park Hotel (now the Payal Club) and beyond that, on the right, is the junction with Mount Pleasant (then Honeypot Lane).

Ealing Road looking south from opposite the Baptist church in 1923. The junction with Mount Pleasant and the Alperton Park Hotel are in the distance.

Alperton Hall (right) stood on the north side of Stanley Avenue and was bought by Henry Haynes in 1885 shortly after construction. It was later used as a private school and then as the Imperial Yeomanry School, before becoming part of Wembley County Grammar (now Alperton High) School in 1922.

The growth of Alperton was spurred on by the opening of the railway in 1903. The Metropolitan District Line initially opened an electric service between Acton Town and Park Royal and then five days later, on 28 June 1903, the railway was extended to South Harrow and the station, then called Perivale-Alperton, was opened. The station was re-named Alperton (for Perivale and Wembley) on 7 October 1910.

Alperton station, early 1920s. A regular train service to South Harrow commenced on Sunday 28 June 1903 at 8.05 a.m. from South Harrow. The original full week-day service was hourly, with additional trains at peak times.

Alperton station was completely rebuilt to designs by Stanley Heaps (but incorporating features of Charles Holden's stations) for the transfer of services to the Piccadilly line which took place on 4 July 1932. The station was completed in 1933, two years before this photograph was taken. (Copyright of London's Transport Museum Ltd)

Two

Preston

The Harrow Golf Club House, photographed here around 1914 from the embankment of Preston Road. It was redeveloped for houses in what is now Grasmere Avenue, as part of the Preston Park estate built by Clifford Sabey in 1932-34.

A view taken in 1934 of what is now the junction of Preston Hill and The Mall, where the road crosses the Wealdstone Brook.

John Lyon farm, pictured here in the 1950s, was demolished in 1960 and replaced by John Perrin Place. Although the farmhouse had been rebuilt in 1708/9, the earlier building on the site had been the home of John Lyon (1514–1592) yeoman of Preston and founder of Harrow School. In February 1572 he obtained a Royal Charter for the Foundation of a Free Grammar School. Two years before his death he drew up 'Orders, Statutes and Rules' for the School's future government, all of which came into effect with the death of his wife in 1608. The first part of the school in Harrow was completed by 1615.

UXENDON SHOOTING SCHOOL CLUB
NEAR HARROW
TELEPHONE Nº 1 WEMBLEY
TELEGRAMS UXENDON WEMBLEY

The farmhouse at Uxendon stood in what is now Uxendon Hill, and had probably been rebuilt in around 1810. In the nineteenth century its farm land extended to 300 acres. By 1900 a shooting club had established itself here and the farm hosted the clay pigeon shoots of the 1908 Olympic Games. The Shooting School survived until around 1929. Thereafter the Metropolitan Line extension (now the Jubilee Line) was built across the grounds and the site was opened up for housing development. An earlier farmhouse on this site had been the home of the Bellamy family, implicated in the Babington plot of 1586. By 1608 the Bellamy estates had passed to Richard Page (d. 1642).

The surviving outbuildings at Uxendon farm in April 1929, the farm having been demolished. (Brent Archive)

The houses shown here in Preston Road in the 1930s were built shortly after the coming of the clay pigeon shooting contests of the Olympic Games to Uxendon in 1908. The halt, opened here on the Metropolitan Railway on 21 May 1908, improved accessibility to this part of Wembley. The halt was built on the east side of the railway bridge. The old Preston Road, shown surviving the building of the new road, has generally become landscaped areas or slip roads. In this case a roundabout has been created at the junction with The Avenue. (Photograph courtesy of the GLC)

Carlton Avenue East near Preston Road is seen here in the 1930s, with newly laid grass verges, pavements, planted saplings and, of course, the absence of traffic.

Four Minutes from Preston Road Station.
(BETWEEN WEMBLEY PARK & HARROW.)

Surrounded BY CHARMING COUNTRY WALKS & Rural Scenery.

PARTIES WELL CATERED F on Reasonab Terms

SPORT GROUND

PRESTON TEA GARDENS & REFRESHMENT ROOMS.
Proprietor. G. TIMMS.

This restful rear garden scene is at the Preston Tea Gardens, founded at Preston House at the top of Preston Hill in around 1880 by George Timms (c. 1834–1899). The business was taken over by his son, George, and was a popular stopping off point, even for the local policeman on his beat. (Brent Archive)

This view takes in the Preston Tea Rooms at the top of Preston Hill, looking south along Preston Road from the junction with Woodcock Hill. Preston Road was widened and straightened in the early 1930s and a new station was built at that time, being completed by February 1932. (Photograph courtesy of the GLC)

Three
Sudbury

A view down The Mall from above the Swan Inn, which is at the bottom right corner. The inn originally lay on the edge of Sudbury Common and, dating back to at least 1786, enjoyed popularity as a coaching stop. Like a number of its contemporaries it suffered the fate of being burnt down and was rebuilt in its present form in the 1890s. It has currently been renamed the Sudbury Inn, although the buses, like the trams before them, continue to terminate at the Swan.

Sudbury Court Farm was one of the most important of Lord Northwick's farms, consisting of 380 acres in the nineteenth century. Though much altered, parts of the building seen here dated back to the seventeenth century, though the cellar appeared to be that of an earlier building, possibly that described in 1547 as 'a mansion house meet for a farmer'.

Plans for the improvement of Sudbury Court Farm in 1842 showed a large room known as the 'court room' where the manor courts must have been held. For the first half of the nineteenth century Sudbury Court Farm was in the hands of the Hill family from Pinner. They were succeeded by Henry Green, and the Perrin family succeeded him in 1900. It was Edward Perrin who sold the farm in 1956. The farm survived on the north side of Sudbury Court Road until 1957, when Percy Bilton Ltd commenced the Kenelm Close housing estate on the site.

The view down Sudbury Court Road towards Watford Road (then Pinner Road), *c.* 1915. In the distance is Sudbury Farm which was run by the Perrin family from 1851, but Mervyn Chute was the farmer when this picture was taken. Part of the farmland survives today as public open space known as 'The Pimple'.

Sudbury Court Road in the 1930s at the junction with Elms Lane, showing the surviving eighteenth and early nineteenth century cottages.

Possibly named after the elm trees which lined the access from Sudbury common (Harrow Road), this was an important farm which was linked to Sudbury Court and its court room by an ancient lane (Elms Lane). On the site were medieval buildings which may have included the principal residence of the Archbishop of Canterbury, until Headstone replaced it in the fourteenth century. Hundred Elms farmhouse, seen here, was a rebuild of around 1840. The outbuilding to the left, which is of around 1550, has recently been converted into a house.

SVDBVRY. HARROW.

Hundred Elms farmhouse was later sold off and the farm buildings converted into a milk depot for Unigate. The attractive set of picture tiles record the yard as it was. The site was re-developed in 1991/92 for housing by Metropolitan Housing Trust, and building works were preceded by an archaeological excavation. The old buildings have been retained.

Opposite Priory Avenue, on the Harrow Road, was Sudbury Priory, seen here from the garden in the 1890's. The house was built in 1828 and the site re-developed in the 1950s.

Elms Lane as seen from its junction with Harrow Road, at which there are farm workers cottages from around 1860-1870.

Elms Lane as a country lane, a character it tries to preserve to the present day.

Harrow Road from St Andrew's church towards Elms Lane and the Swan Inn as seen in the late 1920s. St. Andrew's church was consecrated by the Lord Bishop of London on 20 March 1926. It is a barn-like church with an impressive interior designed by W. Charles Waymouth.

Edwin Butler initially ran the grocer's and post office at 791 Harrow Road, Sudbury but moved to The Poplars nearby. He served on Wembley Council for forty years until 1943 and was the first Mayor of the newly formed Borough of Wembley in 1937.

The open space at the junction of Harrow and Watford Roads was held in trust following Sir William Perkin's death in 1907. It was eventually purchased by Wembley Council in 1920 for £1,825 and opened as Sudbury Recreation Ground. The land lay opposite Butler's shop, and was officially renamed as Butler's Green following Butler's death in 1945, to commemorate his service to the Council. He had been a keen advocate on the Council of purchasing open space for public use.

This view from Crick's shop down The Mall to the bridge carrying the Great Central Railway dates from 1907, and shows the Edwardian village character of the centre along the south-west side of the Harrow Road.

For a period of fifteen years from 1889 the Sudbury shop keeper, Ruben Williams, employed Arthur Crick as Sudbury's hansom cab driver. Thereafter, Crick took over the general store, a service which proved popular and, after 1910, convenient for Sudbury's tram terminus at the Swan roundabout, as he used to serve teas to the drivers of the tram cars.

The tram terminus in the 1920's. The original photograph was retouched before publication as a postcard so that the tram appears without tram lines and wires.

Waiting at the tram terminus at the Swan in the 1930s.

The tram terminus outside the Swan looking north. (Brent Archive)

Rugby Avenue with its neat pavements, grass verges and lack of traffic. It forms part of an estate of roads with college names developed for British Freehold Investments Ltd in 1920, although development of individual plots was still occurring in 1930.

The Poplars, photographed before 1909. Once used by a vivisectionist, it became the home of Edwin Butler and survives in altered form as 773 Harrow Road, occupied in part, at time of writing, by Sudbury Supermarket.

Station Approach, Sudbury, which leads up to the station, was built on the Hundred Elms estate. Housing plans for the odd numbers were prepared for W.H. Watts of Willesden in 1915; the evens were built for J.F. Langer in the early 1920s. The impressive station building now at the head of the cul-de-sac was built to innovative designs by Charles Holden and was opened in July 1931, ready for the transfer of services to the Piccadilly Line in 1932. This picture shows the original 1903 station building.

Sir William Henry Perkin (1838-1907) who discovered aniline dyes, was a scientist of international repute and a resident of Sudbury for fifty years. He was also a keen evangelist and was responsible for starting the Methodist Mission in Sudbury. Chestnut Avenue recalls the name of his residence – The Chestnuts – which stood nearby.

Members of Sir William Perkin's outdoor staff. 'Brummy' Billy Dear, the odd-job-man, is standing. Seated from left to right are James Cady, coachman; William Bignall, under-gardener; and Mr. Nayler, gardener.

A view looking towards Sudbury along the Harrow Road with Crabs House on the right, now Barham Park offices and reception rooms. The property appears to have been built in the late 1700s for James Crab who, in 1801, sold the house and its twenty-four acres of land to John Copland (*c.* 1760-1843), then purser on His Majesty's Ship Malta. On the left is Sudbury Park Farm, one of Barham's model dairy farms.

The Harrow Road at the 'Old Court', now Barham Park. The tram service seen here was open to St John's Road, Wembley, in April 1908. The rebuilding of the railway bridge in the High Road was needed before the tram service could be extended and was only accomplished after many delays. The tram lines reached a new terminus opposite the Swan Inn by August 1910, and the service was opened to Warwick Crescent in September, and then through to Paddington on 6 December 1910.

The Harrow Road at Sudbury approaching the Barham Park entrance on the right-hand side before 1920.

The Harrow Road at Barham Park, Sudbury, *c.* 1914.

John Copland came to Crab's House, Sudbury, in 1801. On his death in 1843, he left his estate to his two daughters, Anne (1792-1872) and Frances (d. 1870). These two philanthropic ladies laid the basis for much of Wembley Central's early growth. They gave the site of St John's church in 1846 and founded the Church School in 1849, both of which they continued to support. Frances gave the land for the Workmen's hall in 1869 and Anne, seen here, founded the Village hospital in 1871.

General Robert Fitzgerald Crawford (1809-1895), an officer of the Royal Artillery, acquired the house and 150 acre Copland estate on the death of Anne Copland in 1872 providing he adopted the name of Copland, which he did by hyphenating it with his own. Crawford moved, socially and spiritually, into the place the Copland sisters had occupied. Between 1894 and 1897 the General, his wife and two of his five sons died and the survivors left the district. On his death in 1895, part of his lands – called the Harrowdene estate – was sold off for housing, thereby effecting a direct connection between North Wembley and Wembley Central.

George Titus Barham (1860-1937) pictured here was the son of Sir George Barham (1836-1913), dairy farmer and founder in 1868 of the Express Country Milk Supply Company, renamed the Express Dairy in 1882, with Titus as joint Managing Director. Barham senior came to live at Crab's House, Sudbury in around 1880, acquiring the Copland estate in 1895. Titus became Chairman of the Express Dairy on the death of his father in 1913. Apart from his philanthropy, Titus succeeded in building up one of the largest dairy businesses in the world at the time. He served on Wembley Council for three years and in 1937 accepted the invitation to become the Borough's first mayor. He died however on the very day that the Charter of Incorporation was to have been sealed.

Barham Park Mansion, to which only the garden balustrades now survive, was originally built for the Copland sisters, probably in the 1850s, after the death of their father in 1843. It was first named Sudbury Lodge and was later re-named as Sudbury Park. Later still, it became the residence of the Barham family and it was Titus Barham who, in 1937, left the Mansion, its grounds and museum collection for the benefit and use of the citizens of Wembley. Its condition however deteriorated during the Second World War when it was used by the Civil Defence and it was eventually demolished in 1956/1957, despite public protests.

Looking north along Watford Road from Vale Farm just after the houses had been built.

The Mitre public house. Both old and new buildings are seen together here on the east side of Watford Road in 1933. First built for the brewer, Thomas Clutterbuck in 1756, the new pub was added in 1933 but demolished in 2000/2001 for retirement flats by McCarthy and Stone, called Bishop's Court. The pub name recalled the earlier connection of Sudbury with the Archbishops of Canterbury.

A delivery boy from the Vale Farm dairy, *c.* 1910. Milk was ladled from the large churn into the small cans. Vale Farm dated back to at least the eighteenth century, and was owned by the millionaire Samuel Palmer – of biscuit fame – in late Victorian times. A late Victorian, early Edwardian replacement 'farmhouse' survives on the site.

The entrance to Vale Farm showing the farm house and the Wembley Sports Ground in the 1930s.

The thirty-three and a half acres of Vale Farm Sports Ground were purchased by Wembley Urban District Council from E. & F. Toley for public playing fields in 1928 and 1931. The swimming pool shown here – the first public pool in Wembley – was opened in April 1932, having been built at a cost of £17,000. (Brent Archive)

Vale Farm Pool in 1964. The open-air pool seen here was replaced by the current two indoor pools on which work commenced in April 1979, at a cost of about £750,000.

The signpost to 'Harrow and Greenford' and to 'Wembley, Willesden and London' gives a clue to this early family outing in Pinner Road (now Watford Road), being at the junction with Sudbury Court Road.

Watford Road in the late 1920s or early 1930s, looking north to Northwick Park from near Carlton Avenue West.

Bridgewater Road was built in the late 1920s, early 1930s, as part of Wembley's Town Planning Scheme. Known at the time as the Sudbury Spur, it straightened and in places by-passed Green Lane, an old country lane whose original alignment survives in part in Clifford Road. The view looks south-east from the junction with Whitton Avenue East to One Tree Hill in the distance.

Cooper's Cottages in 1939/40 with the commencement of demolition. The intense development of cottages started shortly after 1817 with the remainder finished by 1852. The site was cleared for an extension to Sudbury Primary School.

Clyde Cottages lay on the west side of Pinner Road (now Watford Road) just south of Cooper's Cottages and Sudbury Primary School. The General Dealer – Ell's in 1906 – was known as the 'Cyclists' Rest'.

Four
Wembley

The original village of Wembley with its High Street stood, and still stands, on Wembley Hill, on the summit of which is the 'Green Man'. The timber framed property, seen here in 1852, had been a pub since 1722. In 1837 it was described as 'a favourite Sunday resort for a respectable class of people. The grounds command a very extensive panoramic view of the surrounding countryside.'

The present Green Man was rebuilt of more durable brick after the original pub was burnt to the ground in 1906. The attractive Edwardian replacement is shown here shortly after re-opening.

The view from the Green Man looking north to the junction of Park Lane and Wembley Hill Road. Wembley Park lodge is hidden in the trees. Note the outbuildings of Elm Tree Farm on the left.

The Greyhound stood at the end of the High Street. The building was in existence in 1810 and had become a beer shop by 1841. It was demolished in 1929 when the licence was transferred to a new building on the Harrow Road. This view probably dates from the 1920s.

The interior of the old Greyhound on Wembley Hill in 1929 shows the problem of lack of space.

Outside the Greyhound on Cup Final day in 1923, when clearly the limited size of the premises couldn't take the crowds.

The new Greyhound pub was built at the junction of Oakington Manor Drive and Harrow Road at the entry into the Wembley Hill Garden Suburb. It was opened in 1929 having been built to designs by the architect, E.B. Musman. An attractive and stylish pub, but one that attracted opposition to its first licence from local residents who feared rowdy public behaviour.

Oakington Park, later becoming Oakington Manor farm, was leased from around 1862 by Sir Patrick Talbot, the son-in-law of the Earl of Derby, who with the Countess were visitors to Wembley. Talbot played an active part in Wembley's affairs until he left in around 1883, and today is recalled by Talbot Road, near St. John's church where he was a church warden. E.H. Sherren became the tenant in November 1884 of the farm's 375 acres. This photograph was taken in July 1934.

Walter Ernest Sherren, seen here in July 1934, succeeded his father in around 1905 and was the farmer, dairyman and pig breeder at Oakington Manor farm until 1938. At that time the landowner, Sir Audley Neeld, proposed to preserve the house as a library and institute and conveyed this and land about it, along with forty-four acres alongside the River Brent to the Council.

Opposite: The River Brent on the borders of Wembley at Monks Park, near the clinic, in June 1934. In 1913, Sir Audley Dallas Neeld proposed to develop his Tokyngton estate with the agreement of his estate's trustees and the Council. One of the trustees lived at Monks Park in Corsham, Wiltshire, after which Wembley's local shopping parade and suburb was named.

Oakington Manor Farm shortly before demolition. Wembley Council was less appreciative of the house it had been given, and in 1939 it was blown up and set on fire as an A.R.P. exercise.

Oakington Manor Drive, pictured here in 1935, was one of the main tree-lined avenues of the Wembley Hill Garden Suburb, laid out by Neeld's development company, Wembley Hill Estates, in 1914-1924.

In 1845, the Copland sisters took advantage of an Act of 1831 'for building and promoting the building of additional churches in populous parishes' by providing a site in Sudbury. In 1846 the 'Particular District of St. John the Evangelist' came into being and the church was built to designs by Sir George Gilbert Scott, partnered by W.B. Moffat. The dedication may commemorate the name of the donors' father.

High Road, Wembley, from the corner with Lancelot Road in around 1902. The shopping area is beginning to expand with the Railway Hotel and the parade of shops appearing on the right.

High Road, Wembley, at the end of the nineteenth century, from near Ealing Road looking towards the station. (Brent Archive)

Looking east along High Road, Wembley, *c.* 1905, from St John's Road before the trams.

The High Road showing the station on the right before the First World War.

High Road, Wembley, from the station looking westwards to Ealing Road, between 1910 and 1914. (Brent Archive)

The Peace Celebrations in Wembley High Road, held on 19 July 1919. Titus Barham is the figure on horseback.

The Co-op butchers at 84-86 High Road, Wembley, c. 1937, where Dixons is today. (Brent Archive)

High Road, Wembley, in 1920 looking westwards towards the Marks & Spencer store.

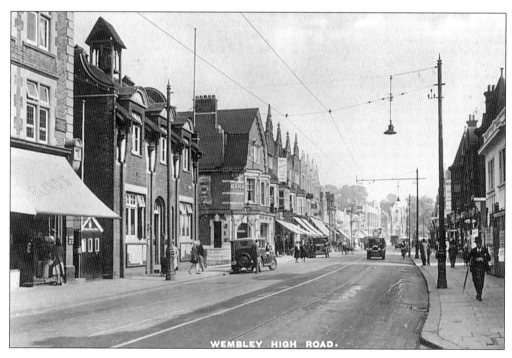

High Road, Wembley, in 1924 looking eastwards from the Council offices at the corner of St John's Road. Barclay's bank is still at the corner.

High Road, Wembley, looking eastwards from the Woolworth's store at the corner of London Road.

Wembley Urban District Council was created in 1895. The offices, seen here in 1935 celebrating the Silver Jubilee of King George V, stood at the corner of High Road and St John's Road.

Looking north up Ealing Road towards the High Road, c. 1930.

Station Grove in 1963, before the demolition of the houses.

High Road, Wembley, looking east from near Ealing Road in 1957.

Wembley Central station and shopping parades in 1957. The station's name was changed from 'Wembley for Sudbury' to 'Wembley Central' in time for the Olympic Games on 5 July 1948.

The coal yard behind the High Road shops in 1962. The crane beyond was being used in the construction of the British Home Stores building and the coal yard itself was redeveloped as Wembley Central Square in 1963-65 to designs by Ardin and Brookes.

There have been five different Post Office buildings in Wembley to date. The first, a sub-post office had appeared in 1878 opposite the steps to Station Grove. This moved after 1895 to where this photograph was taken at 1a Totnes Terrace, later No. 82, now No. 484 High Road. Probably by March 1906 it had moved to new premises which are now part of the site of Woolworth's.

The Workmen's hall was built on the south side of High Road, Wembley, west of its junction with Park Lane in 1869, on land given by Frances Copland. It was the home of the Wembley Institute from that date until 1930 when it was demolished to make way for the development of shops, now 411–417 High Road.

Although the site was occupied in Tudor times, Wembley Orchard, pictured here, had appeared during Queen Victoria's reign. It was demolished in around 1910, and the Wetherspoon pub and adjoining shops on the south side of Wembley High Road (opposite Chesterfield House) now occupy the site. The post office, now the Old Post Office pub, was built in its garden in 1921.

Wembley Smithy had been founded by Charles Thomas and Son – blacksmith, farrier and coach builder – by 1899. The site is still connected with transport, being a petrol filling station adjoining Brent House.

There had been a Wembley House in the sixteenth century, but this was not necessarily on the same site of the early nineteenth century property of that name seen here. This Wembley House, pictured in around 1900, stood on the site of Copland School, and the estate included twenty-seven acres run as a dairy farm. It was occupied in the 1870s by John Woolley, a City stockbroker whose family were solicitors and land agents. He was succeeded by Colonel Topham who proposed the redevelopment of the site, prior to the First World War. The house survived the residential development of the estate by J.C. Isaacs, by being converted by 1915 into a 'ladies' and 'boys' school. Wembley House was acquired by Middlesex County Council for education purposes in 1936 and was eventually demolished.

Wembley House – the site of Copland school – seen from the landscaped grounds in around 1900. (Brent Archive)

Wembley Hill School in 1928. This was the new County Council School built next to Wembley House in 1926, with Miss Ada Hayes as Senior Mixed School Headmistress and Miss Lambert as headmistress of the juniors and infants. The school was demolished by a flying bomb in the war and its site, along with that of Wembley House, was redeveloped as a large Secondary School and opened as Copland School in 1952.

Wembley Triangle in around 1905, with St Joseph's Roman Catholic church on the left.

The shops on the south side of the Harrow Road, seen here at Wembley Triangle, were built just before 1914 when this photograph was probably taken.

William 'Jumbo' Ecclestone, builder, local publican and former heavyweight boxer, publicized his size to his advantage by incorporating his photograph into his letterhead, from which this picture from around 1904 comes. Weighing in at between thirty-five and thirty-seven stones, he travelled in a pony and trap with huge weights in the opposite seat. Ecclestone Place was named after him.

A small brick Roman Catholic church had been erected at Wembley Hill on the south side of the Harrow Road in 1901, and was to prove too small for the congregations. It was replaced by the present church which was built in 1956-57 and consecrated by Cardinal Hulme in 1976. This photograph was taken in 1963, just prior to the commencement of work on the nine storey building of Brent House.

An Act of 1898 empowered the Great Central Railway to build a line of some 6.25 miles between Neasden and Northolt, but it was not until November 1901 that the contract for the construction of the line was placed with Thomas Oliver and Sons of Rugby. The line was opened to goods traffic in November 1905, so that the construction of the line across Oakington, shown here, probably dates from about 1902/1903.

The Great Central was opened through Wembley Hill to goods traffic in November 1905, through to South Harrow for passengers on 1 March 1906, and through to Northolt on 2 April 1906. For this, a station was built on the east side of Wembley Hill Road. The site chosen adjoined an access drive (now part of South Way) to Oakington Farm. Wembley Hill Station, shown here, is now called Wembley Stadium station.

The Great Central Line shown here at Wembley Hill was the last mainline to enter London. A single track spur from it was constructed by the Great Central (although opened on 28 April 1923 by its successor, the London & North Eastern) to serve the first Wembley FA Cup Final.

Wembley Hill Road and the station forecourt are seen here, with the station master's house and the single storey lodge house to Oakington Manor Farm beyond. (Brent Archive)

The construction of the Great Central Railway across Wembley Hill involved a mile long cutting up to 18m (60ft) in depth. A 9m (30ft) high retaining wall was constructed to support the base of the cutting. In February 1918 the land slipped, fracturing the wall and pushing up the land and tracks in front of it. In 1918-1920 additional land was acquired to reduce the gradient on the north side of the cutting.

A countrified Park Lane, photographed in 1910, the year before the primary school – the first Council School in Wembley – was opened.

King Edward VII Park, for which the adjoining road was re-named Park Lane, was laid out to compensate Wembley residents for the loss of the parkland of Wembley Park, which was being developed as a high class residential garden suburb. Its twenty-six acres were purchased in 1913 for £8,050, and were officially opened on 4 July 1914 by Queen Alexandra in memory of her late husband. This photograph shows the playground.

King Edward VII Park: the see-saw in active use on opening day on 4 July 1914.

The bandstand in King Edward VII Park with Park Lane Primary School, which opened in 1911, preceding the housing opposite which was built in 1912-15.

OLD COTTAGES AT WEMBLEY PARK
MIDDLESEX.

Rickyard Cottages seen here in 1905, the year before their demolition. They stood on the east side of Wembley Hill Road, now the site of Nos 132-136, to the north of Wembley Park Lodge. There was a building here called Upright's tenement in the fifteenth century.

The crossroads of Park Lane and Wembley Hill Road, with Wembley Park Lodge in 1933. Note the lack of traffic.

At the entrance of what is now Clarendon Gardens, at the junction of what was Wembley Hill Road and Park Lane (called Blind Lane before the park), stood Elm Tree Farm, featured here. It was leased by the Read family from 1857, but who resided at the house here from 1874 until they emigrated to Australia in 1922. Once again, occupation of the site dated back to the fifteenth century.

Queens Court, shown under construction, formed part of Comben & Wakeling's estate adjoining King Edward VII 's park, which was built along garden suburb lines as part of the Wembley Planning Scheme in 1926–1929.

Wembley Farm at the East Lane and Preston Road crossroads in winter. It became known as Padfield's Farm, a name that is now recalled by a nearby block of flats.

Wembley Farm seen here in around 1900 was built in East Lane, near its junction with Preston Road, on land owned by the Page family in the early part of the nineteenth century. From at least 1811 until 1874 it was occupied by the Read family, and they were succeeded as tenants by the Padfield's who were dairy farmers. The Wembley Park United Reformed church now stands on the site.

FORTY FARM, WEMBLEY.

J. H. & Co's Series

Forty Farm, *c.* 1910. Located by the Wealdstone brook at Forty Green, on what is now Forty Avenue, it was known as 'Pargraves' from medieval times. By 1892 Henry Rich was living there; the Rich brothers were renowned for their horses, hence the composition of the photograph, and they put on polo matches in Wembley Park. Later in its life it was called South Forty and Lower Forty Farm.

Built by local builder George Cloke, and completed on 27 May 1927, the Century Tavern has at the time of writing been replaced by a block of flats by Crest Nicholson, to be called Century House. It was named after the Century Sports Ground whose headquarters in 1928 were nearby at Lower Forty Farm.

WEMBLEY PARK DRIVE FROM THE STATION.   J. H. & Co's Series

Wembley Park Drive and bridge over the Wealdstone (or Lidding) brook, seen from Wembley Park station, c. 1920. Shops and houses are beginning to appear on the right and a glimpse of Wembley Park is provided on the left.

Premises at the bridge in North Wembley before East Lane was widened and straightened.

The Hop Bine appeared by 1871: an attractive two storey building with ground floor bay windows and window boxes above, shown here with regular customers in 1925. The present building, now called the Bootsy Brogan, was built on the site in 1931-1932.

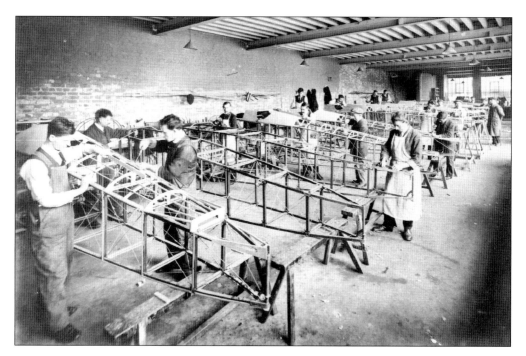

In the communal war effort which followed the outbreak of the First World War, a number of manufacturing firms changed their output to component parts for aircraft. Hooper's, the motor and coach body builders, came to North Wembley in 1917 and a new factory and forty acres of land for a flying ground were provided, along with railway sidings. The manufacture of Sopwiths is seen here. The site was taken over by the GEC in 1922. (Brent Archive)

The General Electric Company acquired Hooper's site and in the following year, in 1923, the Hirst laboratories were opened. Further expansion gave rise to a site extending over sixty-five acres.

The Norfolk Arms was built on Llanover Road in the 1860s; its first proprietor was born in Norfolk! The pub is shown here with Billy Sampson as an inset. Sampson had become the licensee here in 1906 and left in 1932, three years after its rebuilding. He was known throughout the area for his interest in sport, and especially boxing. Many famous boxers, like Kid Lewis, trained in his gymnasium at the back of the pub.

These cottages stood on the south side of East Lane on the site of what is now Nos 63-69. Photographed here in 1914, they were built as labourers' cottages early in the nineteenth century.

84

Five

Wembley Park

The marriage of Susanna Newman and Richard Page in 1745 united the Page estates of Harrow and Wembley. In 1771 the Wembley estate passed to their eldest son, Richard (1748-1803), who in around 1787 chose a new manor house for himself. By stopping up a highway called Botnall Lane he was able to provide an existing large Georgian house called Wellers with a substantial private parkland. This was to become the new Wembly Park Mansion, seen here, and in around 1792 he engaged the landscape architect Humphry Repton to improve the park's landscape, and improve the appearance of the house.

Repton's proposals for Wembly Park, including thinning the plantations, follies, an entrance lodge house in Wembley Hill Road and a 'prospect tower' on Barn Hill, were published as one of his 'Red' books – so called because they were clad in red Moroccan leather. He considered that 'within so short a distance from London…Wembly is as quiet and retired at seven miles distance as it could have been at seventy'. Work was underway on the landscaping by May 1793. This view is over Wembly Park from Barn Hill.

The grasslands of the private estate of Wembly Park, photographed from the Mansion House in about 1880.

Richard Page died in 1803 but appears to have left Wembly Park a year earlier, without having implemented Repton's designs for the house. Ownership passed to John Gray (1747–1828) from Winchmore Hill, London, who between 1811 and 1814 spent some £14,000 on extending and renovating the house in a style of considerable elegance. This is a rare photograph of Wembley Park Mansion, taken in 1880 in the time of Revd J.E. Gray (1800–1887). The house was demolished in 1908 and Manor Drive now passes through its site.

The entrance lodge to Wembly Park was built to Repton's 'cottage ornee' designs, probably in 1793, and still survives in Wembley Hill Road at the junction with Wembley Park Drive. In its original attractive setting, it was the subject of many photographs and postcard views.

Glimpses of the Wembley parkland through the gates revealed a world of splendid seclusion, whilst the growth of suburban Edwardian London had almost reached its borders.

Hillcrest stood at what is now the junction of Manor Drive and Wembley Hill Road. It was a survival (until around 1920) of the former Wembly Park being built as a dower house for Sarah Gray (1774–1854) who outlived her husband, John Gray, by twenty-six years. The site was redeveloped for houses by the local builders, Comben & Wakeling, in 1923.

The name of Barn Hill occurs as Bardonhill in 1547. From the top, 85m above sea level, there are fine views to the north and south which Repton appreciated when he sited a 'prospect tower' here. A guide book refers to the tower or folly in existence in 1820, and a map of 1819 shows the pond at the summit. The origin of the pond shown here is uncertain but may have been part of Repton's proposals implemented in 1793. (Brent Archive)

The road to Wembley in January 1898. A scene – possibly of Forty Lane – which was typical of Wembley's country lanes.

A postcard which advertised the arrival of the Metropolitan railway. Extended through to Harrow in August 1880 the railway had passed through Wembley Park for which the then owner, Revd John Gray, sold some forty-seven acres of parkland. The railway skirted Wembley village and only opened a station at Wembley Park because of the new pleasure ground on 12 May 1894.

Building work on Wembley Tower began on 13 June 1893, and the first platform at 47m (155 feet) was complete by September 1895. The park was officially opened in May 1894 and attracted 120,000 people in the 1895 season. Public enthusiasm waned however; the tower construction already behind schedule halted at the first platform and the Metropolitan Tower Construction Company finally went into voluntary liquidation in 1899.

GENERAL VIEW
OF
WEMBLEY PARK,
AS SEEN FROM RAILWAY STATION,
SHEWING TOWER AS IT WILL
APPEAR WHEN COMPLETE.
TOTAL HEIGHT 1150 FEET.

SKETCH PLAN
SHEWING PROXIMITY
OF PARK TO STATION.
FROM BAKER ST

In 1889, two years after Gray's death, the 280 acres of the Wembley Park estate was sold to the Chairman of the Metropolitan Railway, Sir Edward Watkin (1819–1901), at a price of nearly £32,930. He proposed a spectacular pleasure ground with sporting facilities, ornamental lake and gardens, fountain, pavilions, bandstands and, above all, a tower to rival the Eiffel, newly opened in Paris. The tower engineer was Sir Benjamin Baker. The foundations were laid by Joseph Firbank (who also had the contract to build Wembley Park station – opened in 1894) and the tower structure above ground was built by Heenan & Froude (of Blackpool Tower fame).

Wembley Park: the Tower seen from the lake, c. 1902. The vista is equivalent to a view of the Stadium today from the roundabout in Wembley Park Drive, except that buildings are in the way.

The IBSA (Inanimate Bird Shooting Association) championships were held in the park in June 1898. This presumably included clay pigeon shooting.

The Polytechnic Harriers at Wembley Park in 1896.

An attractive fountain formed part of the landscaped grounds in front of Wembley Tower, photographed in autumn 1897.

Visitors in Victorian dress on the Wembley Tower platform in autumn 1897.

At 47m (155ft) above ground the first platform afforded views over Wembley's countryside. The photograph here, taken in 1897, looks towards Barn Hill.

Wembley Tower (or Watkin's Folly as it became known) was dismantled and removed in 1907 by Heenan & Froude, the foundations being finally blown up on 9 September 1907.

Taken just before the First World War, this scene shows the lawn mowers at work on the Wembley Park Golf course with the craters of the Wembley Tower legs still evident. This scene is where the middle of the Stadium pitch is today.

A view of the eastern edge of Wembley Park taken from in front of the tower site, c. 1910. From the refreshment house in the left foreground the view takes in a small bandstand, the main pavilion in the distance and the chimneys of Neasden power station. (Photo courtesy of the GLC)

The Wembley Park Golf course is seen from the Tower site to Barn Hill, with Refreshment Rooms in view, c. 1914. Wembley Park Station is in the middle distance, hidden by the trees.

The Wembley Park Golf Club House, pictured here around 1915, looking south-east across the slope of Barn Hill. It was situated between what is now The Crossways and Barn Way, to the rear of Barn Rise. It was demolished in the 1920s.

A family outing probably in Forty Avenue enjoying the lane with its lack of traffic.

Bridge Road when it was a footpath in 1920, passing through the belt of trees at the junction with Forty Lane.

Forty Lane (now Forty Avenue) at 'Forty Green', where the road crosses the Wealdstone Brook.

Forty Avenue (then Forty Lane) looking east towards Wembley Park, before 1920.

100

The Empire Stadium was built for the British Empire Exhibition which was held at Wembley Park in 1924-25. The Exhibition was to attract twenty-seven million people to an area of countryside for which local rural lanes had to be widened and straightened and the scheme was officially launched at a meeting at the Mansion House on 7 June 1920. At the time this photograph was taken in May 1922 the oval shape of the emerging Stadium is clearly discernible, but so too are the holes from the footings of the four legs of Wembley Tower which would have been sited in the middle of the pitch! (Copyright of Simmons Aerofilms Ltd)

The total cost of constructing and equipping the stadium was just over £507,000. During construction, the strength of the floors was tested by the application of loads of sand and by a battalion of 1,200 men who marched, stood and sat in unison. Room was provided for 120,000 spectators however the attendance of the King and Queen, just after the marriage of the Duke of York to Lady Elizabeth Bowes-Lyon, helped to attract about 200,000. Famous for its twin domed towers and bastion features the building has become a symbol of national football. This photograph shows the Stadium under construction in September 1922 and what appears to be the stacks for the brick and lime works in Willesden in the distance. (Copyright of Simmons Aerofilms Ltd)

The Exhibition grounds covered 216 acres. Sir John Simpson (1858-1933) and Maxwell Ayrton (1874-1960) were appointed architects and Owen Williams the site engineer. In January 1922 Sir Robert McAlpine were appointed contractors. The first turf was cut at Wembley by the Duke of York on 10 January 1922. Nearly 2,000 men were engaged in constructing the Exhibition buildings during 1923 and 1924. The Palaces are shown under construction here in 1922/23 with the Palace of Industry in the foreground. Olympic Way now crosses from top left to mid right. (Copyright of Simmons Aerofilms Ltd)

A west/east view of the heart of the Exhibition grounds across the lakes leading up to the India Pavilion, with Barnhill Road in the top left and Neasden power station at the top centre.

The Exhibition's official theme was 'to stimulate trade, to strengthen the bonds that bind the Mother Country to her sister states and daughter nations, to bring all into closer touch the one with the other, to enable all who owe allegiance to the British flag to meet on common ground and to learn to know each other. It is a family party to which every part of the Empire is invited, and at which every part of the Empire is represented.' This picture of the Exhibition, taken in July 1924, shows the main pavilions of Canada, Australia, and the domed top of Malaya furthest away to the right. (Copyright of Simmons Aerofilms Ltd)

This aerial view of the Exhibition grounds is taken from above the Palace of Industry and is centred on the Canada Pavilion with the lakes, Australia Pavilion and Stadium in clear view.

The Empire Stadium built in ferro-concrete in 1922-1923 was intended for large scale events such as for choirs, massed bands, displays, pageants, the Tattoo and rodeo. In the event it was completed in time for the FA Cup final of 1923 in which Bolton Wanderers beat West Ham United 2-0. The start of the match was delayed by forty minutes by the crowds swarming onto the pitch. Order was regained through the efforts of P.C. George Scorey on a white horse, and by the response of the crowd to the arrival of King George V.

The German airship *Graf Zeppelin* crossed the Stadium during the 1930 Cup Final when Arsenal beat Huddersfield Town 2-0.

Wembley Stadium is seen here just after the war, with the influx of cars beginning to make its mark.

The Palace of Industry viewed from the Australia Pavilion, across the lake (hence Lakeside Way today) with Barn Hill in the distance. The building survives today, but in its heyday provided a vast Exhibition area of Britain's manufactured goods.

In the Palace of Industry there were joint displays by members of each main industry: chemicals – including perfumes; cotton, wool and silk; clocks, jewellery and cutlery; furniture and furnishings; stationery, leather, glass and pottery; music; gas; and building materials. There were also food products, beverages, sports, games and toys; India rubber products and scientific instruments and a special display by Northern Ireland.

The exhibits in the Palace of Engineering were divided into five main groups: ship-building and marine engineering, mechanical and general engineering, (which included exhibits by 300 leading firms showing engines, locomotives, turbines, cranes and heavy machinery), electrical and allied engineering (including switch-gear, transformers and radio receivers); water transport; land transport; and a motor and cycle section.

The lakeside façade of the Palace of Engineering in 1924 with a 'railodok' car and passengers. The floor space of the building exceeded 46,000sq.m. (500,000ft.).

Water transport exhibits in the Palace of Engineering included exhibits of ports and models of steamships and liners. Railways and trams featured in the Land Transport section - railways having celebrated their centenary in 1925. The Motor Transport section was the forerunner of the Motor Show.

The Australian Pavilion covered 5.5 acres and was surrounded by a garden ring of native trees, shrubs and ferns. There were exhibits, models, diagrams and cinema films showing the country's wealth and potential. Machine shearing of sheep was demonstrated hourly and industrial exhibits displayed agricultural, dairy, mining and fishing activities and products.

The Australia and Malaya pavilions as seen from the lake.

The Malaya Pavilion stood in what is now Empire Way and carried the royal colours of Malaya, yellow and white; it was furnished in red and yellow, black and white, and illuminated by Chinese lanterns made in Singapore. It had lofty minarets flanking its dome. The exhibits were arranged in seven sections: Forestry, Fisheries, Mines, Commerce, Agriculture, Arts and Crafts, and Scenery.

Kiosk for the sale of Abdulla cigarettes advertising Turkish Egyptian Virginia tobacco. A native guard is in attendance.

Hong Kong elected to reproduce one of its native streets with twenty-four shops fitted and arranged as would have been seen there. Native workers and merchants busied themselves in silk, silver, ivory, rattan, blackwood and paper. Opposite the shops was a large Chinese restaurant, with Chinese food, waiters and live music.

Guarded by lions and overhung by flags, the British Government Pavilion was built in eight months. On entering, the visitor was confronted by a contour map of the world with model ships plying the oceans. The pavilion had aerial, naval and military displays, and depicted the work of various Government offices. The storming of Zeebrugge was shown in detail, as was the making of a loaf of bread!

At the Burma Pavilion, small gilded bells on the three towers rang in the wind. Inscriptions of welcome at the entrance were in carved and lacquered teak. In the garden was a shrine with a marble Buddha which, with its contents, were made in Rangoon and shipped here. There were exhibits of wood, rice and cereals, and films of the teak forests, oil fields, railways and ruby mines. A Burmese theatre group gave daily performances and two small Burmese elephants could be seen strolling around the grounds. (Brent Archive)

The impressive India Pavilion covered five acres and each of its twenty-seven provinces were represented. Each expressed its own individuality, showing its own wares, arts and crafts. In the theatre were native actors, jugglers and snake charmers. There were models of the railways, the North-West frontier and a reclamation scheme in Bombay, and a jungle exhibit, to which Kings, Viceroys and Rajahs contributed trophies. Exhibits included silks and embroidery, muslin and brocades, brass work and jewels. Virtually every aspect of life seemed to be covered.

The India Pavilion. The guide book observed that 'time passes imperceptibly under the roof of this pavilion, because there are novelties at every turn'.

East Africa exhibits covered countries from the Sudan to Kenya, Uganda, Zanzibar, Mauritius and the Seychelles. Resources, products and crafts were displayed from each, and were little known to the average visitor. The Gold Coast building resembled a castle of the early Danish settlers. The interior consisted of seven panoramic courts including exhibits of cocoa, clothes, wooden idols, diamonds and metal work.

The gateway to a medieval bridge, misnamed London Bridge – which it didn't even resemble, led the way to small shops and displays along the route. It contrasted with the delicately carved buildings of Burma.

Canada's display at the Exhibition covered nearly six acres There were sections devoted to the country's forestry and timber products, food items, machinery and vast mineral wealth. There were murals, panoramic pictures, and extensive photographs including a picture of the great belt of the Western Prairie where model railways were integrated.

Amongst the Canadian dairy exhibits in 1924 was a life-sized model of the Prince of Wales and his horse, made entirely in butter.

There were thirty or forty advertising kiosks in the Exhibition grounds and a wide variety of souvenirs to be purchased to suit every pocket. Here, a salesman is selling off Goss china as the 1925 Exhibition draws to a close.

Nearly fifty acres of ground were devoted to a comprehensive Amusements Park, including a scenic railway, the mile long Grand National Switchback, dance hall, Tutankhamun's tomb (a replica of the recent discovery), fairground, coal mine, water chute, flying machine, rifle range , river caves, the Palace of Neptune – which displayed many varieties of fish – and so on. There were hundreds of games and side shows to tempt the skills of the visitor.

The Exhibition even had a full-sized colliery with its head gear and underground workings complete. A 5.5m (18ft) diameter main shaft (accidentally stumbled across in 1985), nearly 14m (45ft) deep, took visitors down to workshops and accommodation and coal lined galleries were created for the occasion. Pit ponies were in attendance along with ten working miners drawn from the Lancashire, Yorkshire and Nottinghamshire coal fields. Over 900,000 people paid to visit this exhibit in 1924.

The Kingsway was the main pedestrian route between the Palaces of Industry and Engineering, from the gardens in the north, near Wembley Park station, to the lakes beside Engineers Way. The route is now occupied by Olympic Way, which was built and opened for the Olympic Games which were held here in 1948.

Covering 216 acres, the Exhibition site was a vast area for the visiting public and a number of transport systems were on hand to help people get about. These included the Never Stop Railway which ran over three miles and could carry 15,000 people daily. It ran from near Wembley Park station to near the Stadium, and carriages were propelled by an electrically driven revolving spiral which screwed the carriages forward. This photograph shows the northern terminus near what became North End Road in 1925.

The Stronach-Dutton Roadrails system, seen here in 1924, was less successful than the Never Stop Railway. The weight of the train was taken on steel rails whilst the rubber-treaded propulsive wheels operated on the road surface.

119

The Never Stop Railway could reach a top speed of between 16 and 24mph. The compactness of the screw thread determined how fast the cars could travel. The carriages slowed at stations to enable people to walk on and off so that they 'never stopped'! This photograph shows the screw thread.

The remains of the lake and the Stadium in May 1948, prior to the Games.

The Cup tie crowds on 24 April 1926 at the bus station in Wembley Hill Road (now the frontage of York House). The minarets of the Malaya Pavilion are seen in the distance. (Copyright of London's Transport Museum)

A loop off the Great Central Railway enabled trains from Marylebone station to enter the Exhibition grounds at the 'Exhibition' station, behind the India Pavilion. This picture shows the 'Wembley Stadium' station, as it later became, in 1948. The loop line was finally closed on 1 September 1969.

Opposite: Two views of Wembley Park station from Bridge Road in August 1933. The street buildings at Wembley Park station were rebuilt in 1923 in time for the Exhibition crowds. Further internal modifications took place in preparation for the 1948 Olympics. Note the advertisement for the housing by Haymills on the Barn Hill estate. The land had been acquired by them in 1923 and the first roads were laid out in 1926-1929. (Both copyright of London's Transport Museum)

Wembley Stadium on Cup Final day, on 7 May 1955. Note the Welsh Harp Reservoir at the top, the Metropolitan Line and Neasden power station, the Marylebone/High Wycombe Line on the right and, of course, the cars! (Copyright of Simmons Aerofilms Ltd)

The survival of the Stadium after the Exhibition largely rested on the foresight and drive of Sir Arthur Elvin, and it was he who decided to stage ice hockey in Wembley following an England-Canada match in London in 1932. The result was a new indoor Stadium, designed as a swimming pool, but which could be converted into an ice rink and floored over to provide indoor sport. Sir Owen Williams designed the Empire Pool (now the Wembley Arena) and it was built in 1933-1934 at a cost of £200,000. (Copyright of Simmons Aerofilms Ltd)

The Wembley Arena, as it is today, staged the swimming events of the Empire Games in 1934, and the European Championships in 1938, but the pool has not resumed its original function since the Olympic Games seen here in 1948.

Boxing at the Empire Pool during the Olympic Games of 1948.

Lawns Court comprises six part two/ part three storey blocks comprising fifty flats in The Avenue. It was built in the then current 'Moderne' style on the Holland estate of Forty Farm in 1932–1933. The architects were Welch, Cachemaille-Day and Lander. This aerial view was taken in May 1936 and looks towards Preston and Kenton in the distance. (Copyright of Simmons Aerofilms Ltd)

The Town Hall in Forty Lane nearing completion on 2 June 1939. The building was the subject of an architectural competition, of which the sole assessor was Stanley Hamp. The architect, Clifford Strange, was awarded first prize. Wembley Council was granted Borough status at the same time that building works commenced in 1937, and today's municipal offices were completed in wartime. (Copyright of Simmons Aerofilms Ltd)